THE BEST OF
MATT
1993

'You put your left leg in,
your left leg out . . .'

MATTHEW PRITCHETT was voted Granada's *What the Papers Say* Cartoonist of the Year in 1992. He studied at St Martin's School of Art in London and first saw himself published in the *New Statesman* during one of its rare lapses from high seriousness. He has been *The Daily Telegraph's* front-page pocket cartoonist since 1988.

The Daily Telegraph

THE BEST OF

MATT

1993

CHAPMANS

Chapmans Publishers
A Division of the Orion Publishing Group Ltd
Orion House
5 Upper St Martin's Lane
London WC2H 9EA

First published by Chapmans 1993

The right of Matthew Pritchett to be identified as the
author of this work has been asserted by him in accordance
with the Copyright, Designs and Patents Act, 1988

A CIP catalogue record for this book is available
from the British Library

ISBN 1–85592–662–8

Photoset in Meridien Medium
Printed and bound in Great Britain by
The Guernsey Press Co. Ltd, Guernsey, Channel Islands

THE BEST OF

MATT

'In an effort to delay the
Maastricht treaty we're
asking people not to put
forward their clocks'

'*I'm living out one
of my fantasies*'

Madonna's *Sex* was the most hyped book of
recent years. Not everyone thought it very sexy,
however

'And this is the driver's chocolate bar'

'Do you have the feeling that other people are answering more sex surveys than you?'

Even heavier lorries are to be allowed on Britain's roads

More sex surveys than ever were published in 1993 – some said to boost the circulation of ailing magazines

A group of Punjabis offered to airlift relief supplies to recession-hit Stockport

Fines linked to the offender's ability to pay led to some huge – and hugely unpopular – penalties for petty offences

'I'm thinking of giving up this lark and starting an electricity company'

'Read a little bit about it'

Some newly privatised industries announced very large profits – and very large perks for their directors

The Calcutt Report recommended curbs on press intrusion – the press objected vociferously

Plans were mooted to introduce tolls on motorways – as a plane made an emergency landing on one

After a long battle, the government was forced to abandon plans to redevelop Oxleas Wood in South London

Home Affairs

'She gazed dreamily into his blue swimming pool, ran her fingers through his unruly acres, and breathed, I will'

'Don't worry darling. I'm just making sure my secretary doesn't turn to drugs'

Raine Spencer – Barbara Cartland's daughter – married a dashing French count

Princess Diana – Raine Spencer's stepdaughter – spoke to a drugs charity of the need for love and hugs

Home Affairs

'Hello, Ministry of Agriculture? I've just drunk twelve pints of cider and I feel a bit peculiar'

'I heard an oil tanker's run aground. I wonder if it's us'

The Ministry of Agriculture failed to inform the public that high levels of a toxin had been found in apple juice

A supertanker ran aground and broke up off the Shetland Islands, threatening an ecological disaster

Home Affairs

'How marvellous, a woman
up Everest—now she can
tidy the place up a bit'

A loo was installed on Mount Everest to
accommodate the increasing number of climbers
– and the mountain's slopes are now littered
with equipment left by previous expeditions.
Rebecca Stephens became the first British
woman to reach the summit

Home Affairs

'I'm afraid you're too late'

Moves to allow women priests in the Church of England took a decisive step forward

The IRA tried but failed to bomb Canary Wharf – and interrupted production of *The Daily Telegraph*

Home Affairs

'I'm only pollinating deserving flowers that are married'

'What? You mean today's not another bank holiday?'

One-parent families are costing **the** country billions of pounds **in social** security payments, **according** to the government

There were calls – by now traditional every spring – for the British to take fewer holidays

Home Affairs

'I'll show you to your room, sir'

'WOW!'

The prestigious Holbeck Hall Hotel in Scarborough crashed into the sea after a landslide

Home Affairs

'We'll never get a taxi. Let's just buy one of these houses'

'Some people have all the luck'

The property slump continued in England, although in the USA extensive hurricane damage 'moved the market'

Foreign Affairs

'They're genuine Russian
dolls—none of them
fits together'

Dan Quayle – famous for
spelling potato with an 'e' –
lost his job in the US elections

The Russian economy slid
further into chaos as more
Western credits were pumped in

The Budget

'And now I propose to
drown my sorrows for the
tax year 1995-96'

'It's a phased programme.
By 1994-95 we won't be
getting any runs at all'

The March 1993 Budget included tax increases to
be phased in later. England had had a rotten Test
tour of India

The Budget

'Global warming is the
only hope we've got'

There was little good news in the Budget. VAT
would be levied on domestic fuel bills, said the
Chancellor

The Budget

'We're rich—I've lost
my driver's licence'

'It's not a nicotine patch,
it's my bank statement—
it reminds me I can't
afford to smoke'

There were the customary increases in alcohol,
tobacco and transport taxes

Lloyd's

'This probably isn't the time to tell him we're Lloyd's Names'

'DON'T JUMP!'

London Zoo survived a cash crisis – but Lloyd's, famous for its high-tech building with the pipes on the outside, lost vast sums and many Names faced ruin

Privatised Prisons

'Psst, I've hidden a bottle of sun cream inside'

'You treat this place like a privatised prison'

A report from Her Majesty's Chief Inspector of Prisons revealed that remand prisoners at the Wolds spent their time sunbathing and lazing around

Politics

'I wouldn't stand too close to the PM. If anyone is going to be struck by lightning . . .'

'And if David Gower had been Chancellor, none of this would have happened'

The Prime Minister, it was said, was accident-prone and the government's competence was questioned – like that of England's beleaguered cricket team

Politics

'Things get a bit blurred when politicians start talking about the Vision Thing'

'Actually, we thought you'd like to sit up on the platform, Mr Major'

Many people wondered what the government stood for. Did John Major have a vision for Britain – or what it takes to be leader of his party?

Politics

'When I spoke of the need
for tough decisions...'

'We give the impression of
being on the pitch but
not in the game'

Chancellor Norman Lamont finally left the
government in a reshuffle. In his resignation
speech, he said that the government gave the
impression of being in office but not in power –
in the meantime England's soccer squad kept
losing

Politics

'I was a victim of
a charm offensive'

'You can go up to your neck
in hot water with this
watch, Mr Mates'

The small Conservative
majority in the Commons led to
tough tactics by government
whips, particularly over
Maastricht

When it emerged that Northern
Ireland Minister Michael Mates
had given failed tycoon Asil
Nadir a watch as a token of
support, he got into such
trouble that he resigned

Politics

'Mr MacGregor, if you've got a rail privatisation plan, slip it under the door'

'Say what you like about this Government, but they certainly make the privatisations run on time'

Plans to privatise British Rail were mooted by John MacGregor – but exactly how these plans would work remained a tricky question

Politics

'It faints when the pit is about to be mothballed'

'Would you mind if the chairman hid in your cellar for a few weeks?'

There was a furore when British Coal suddenly announced plans for extensive pit closures. The plans were later modified

Can't Pay, Won't Pay

'Call me an old softie, but
I've given in to Mr Major's
plea to limit your pay rise'

'I'm in the private sector,
there's no need to
show restraint'

The recession kept pay rises to a minimum –
although within many of Britain's boardrooms
the gravy train continued

That Family

'My electric toothbrush is picking up an intimate royal conversation'

'I just taped a man, who taped a man, who taped the Prince of Wales'

The scandal of the 'Royal Tapes' left one question unresolved: Who had made them?

That Family

'She's put this down as
office furniture'

'Well, it's one of Her
Majesty's Prisons—she
should pay for it'

Hard times for the Queen as public opinion
persuaded her not only to pay tax, but also to
pay for a substantial part of the damage to
Windsor Castle

That Family

'No, this is not a coach party'

Parts of Buckingham Palace were opened to the public for the first time

That Family

'Climb up this instead'

HIGHGROVE

'. . . Second syllable, first word, rhymes with . . .'

The Queen made history by agreeing to pay income tax

There was much talk of scrambler telephones and other techniques to prevent more royal conversations being bugged

The 'M' Word

'This Maastricht Bill could save us a lot of trouble'

'I've locked my owner inside—he gets so upset about Maastricht'

A crucial Commons vote on the Maastricht Bill was held on 5 November 1992

The 'M' Word

'I can't help wondering how they'll vote in the referendum'

The French narrowly voted 'yes' in a referendum on Maastricht

The 'M' Word

'Let's have another referendum and make it the best of three!'

'Lord Tebbit doesn't want the Continental breakfast'

The Danes voted against Maastricht in a first referendum but then voted in favour on a second – meanwhile Lord Tebbit was at a Tory conference where he made a dramatic anti-Maastricht speech

The 'M' Word

'They should have had a referendum on whether to broadcast this!'

'If I hadn't got out a copy of the Maastricht treaty they would never have left'

Maastricht first bewildered people, then bored them

The 'M' Word

'We watch Red Hot Dutch
every evening—it's the
only channel where they
never mention Maastricht'

'Obscene, meaningless and
infuriating—I'm entering
it for the Turner Prize'

By the summer of 1993, most people would do anything to avoid the dreaded 'M' word. Meanwhile, the annual Turner Prize for art was strongly criticised, and 'Red Hot Dutch', a pornographic satellite TV channel, began beaming into the UK

The 'M' Word

'You answered all twenty questions on Maastricht. Goodness knows whether you were right or not'

'I know you Euro-sceptics, you say one thing when you really mean the opposite'

Few people seemed to know what Maastricht was really about and things got worse when Euro-sceptics voted *for* the Social Chapter in an effort to wreck the whole treaty

BR Regrets . . .

'*I'm trying to beat the train strike—can I vandalise one of your rooms?*'

After much rancour, the government finally selected a route for the Channel tunnel rail link. In the meantime, there were 24-hour rail strikes as a result of BR's privatisation plans

Sporting Times

'Ready? Let's start. . .NO just a minute, GO. . .STOP! This meeting's cancelled'

'We've bought Peter Scudamore this gold watch but it won't start'

Turmoil at the start, when riders failed to respond to a recall flag, led to the Grand National being declared void

Peter Scudamore resigned from the Jockey Club, though not in protest at the Grand National affair

Sporting Times

'Your jockey is in danger of exceeding the 48-hour working week'

'I wasn't expecting a challenge to my leadership'

The government rejected EC proposals to limit Britain's working week to 48 hours

Over the summer, John Major's unpopularity led to speculation that a stalking-horse would be put up against him in a Conservative Party vote

Sporting Times

'I think we should condemn
a little more and understand
a little less'

'Well, judging by how long
they lasted, they must be
from an England batsman'

The year began badly for England's cricket team.
As the Prime Minister talked about getting tough
with juvenile criminals, our batsmen wilted in
the sun in India

Sporting Times

'It's still deuce—you
haven't missed anything'

As England's cricketers struggled to find their
form against Australia, Graham Gooch handed
over as Captain to Michael Atherton. England's
batting had collapsed during the first few Tests

Sporting Times

'It has been decided to widen the bands in which the English and Australian scores are permitted to fluctuate'

'It's the Prime Minister'

During the summer, the ERM was revised to allow its currencies to fluctuate within wider bands – little consolation to England's Test side

The Prime Minister, a keen cricket fan, was overhead calling some of his Maastricht rebels 'B*s!!?ds'

Sporting Times

'Well that's killed the
art of conversation'

By the fourth Test against Australia, miracles
were indeed required by England's cricketers.
Could they make a comeback? Much to
everyone's surprise they did, winning the final
Test

Sporting Times

'I cut myself shaving'

'I heard all the moaning and thought you must be watching Lady Chatterley's Lover'

Andre Agassi played at Wimbledon – with a hairless chest. He claimed that this made him more aerodynamic on court

Anyone who had had enough of grunting competitors at Wimbledon could turn to a newly televised version of *Lady Chatterley's Lover*

Sporting Times

'HELP! It's Prince Philip'

Prince Philip's yacht suffered a collision at the beginning of Cowes Week, though later in the week he went on to win

The long-awaited chess match between Boris Spassky and the mercurial Bobby Fischer began with intensive psychological manoeuvring

School's Out

'You look like you need
a cigarette, sir'

'Well, thank goodness
I didn't get one'

The new national curriculum was criticised by
many teachers, especially plans to publish
league tables of schools' examination results

School's Out

'Don't worry, Miss, I've forgotten all last term's English lessons anyway'

'I've got good news—guess what "boycott" means'

Changes began to be introduced in schools, but teachers boycotted many of the new national curriculum tests

Cops and Robbers

Statistics showed that crime had reached record levels – yet again

The police tried out a new two-handled truncheon – perhaps of appeal to England's unhappy Test batsmen

Cops and Robbers

'It's amazing to think some city kids have never seen a burglary'

'It's very sad—this used to be a tyre and exhaust centre before all the car thefts'

Rural crime began to increase even faster than inner-city crime

Cops and Robbers

'Couldn't we be paid to run
our home as a juvenile
detention centre?'

'I now declare this juvenile
secure unit open'

To combat a wave of juvenile crime, the
government announced plans to open more
secure units for young offenders

Cops and Robbers

'There's an organised group
of insurance companies
preying on people like you'

'The judge called me a
vigilante and gave me
six months'

As crime soared, insurance premiums went up
sharply. A few frustrated citizens took the law
into their own hands

Cops and Robbers

'Police? Can you see with your High Street video camera if the greengrocer has any broccoli?'

To combat thieves, more security cameras were placed in High Streets

The amount of crime in Britain shocked everyone

Cops and Robbers

'And this is the current Marquess of Blandford'

The unhappy Marquess of Blandford was chased
by police and spent a short period in detention.
While in detention, former boxer Mike Tyson
began to reform himself

Cops and Robbers

'That's where the Super fainted when he saw the Sheehy Report'

Plans to reform the police, proposed in the Sheehy Report, went down very badly with the force

Dept X, Whitehall

'Hello GCHQ, Mr Major can't remember what Clinton said about Iraq. Did you tape it?'

GCHQ was revealed to have been bugging the Royals – and perhaps everyone else

'I didn't tell Mrs Rimington she was invited—I assumed she'd find out'

Stella Rimington, the head of MI5, broke new ground when she met MPs for lunch

Sunny Spells

'Well, December has certainly started badly'

A wet winter, a wet spring and a wet summer
did little to enliven spirits

Doctors and Nurses

'And I'm making out a loan
application for you to
take to the bank'

Prescription charges went up yet again. In the
meantime, hospital closures and 'streamlining'
got under way

Hard Times

'I'll put you down as
pessimistic, then?'

The year began with dire economic news

Hard Times

'I've got a nasty feeling that this conference could last longer than my business'

The recession 'bottomed out' with a vengeance

Hard Times

'If we wish upon a star maybe all our dreams will come true'

'No, officer, it wasn't a U-turn, it was a change of emphasis'

EuroDisney in France announced large losses and the future of the complex seemed in doubt

As the pound fluctuated wildly on the foreign exchanges, the government tried to think of another word for U-turn

Hard Times

'We're saved!'

EX HOOVER
EMPLOYEE.
GIVE 10p
AND GET
£5 BACK

The Hoover company offered free air tickets to
customers who bought goods worth more than
£100. So many people applied that the scheme
ended in disaster

Hard Times

'It's going well, Sarge,
he's just made an offer
for my house'

'We got the idea from those
new police speed traps'

A few signs of economic recovery emerged in the
spring, just as speed-trap cameras were installed
on major roads

Hard Times

*'That's an encouraging sign
of an upturn in retail sales'*

Signs of economic recovery continued
throughout the spring and summer, although
some companies, including Barclays Bank,
posted losses and redundancies

Hard Times

'It fell off the
back of a lorry'

'I've been waiting in
all morning for my
redundancy papers'

Leyland DAF was rescued by a management
buy-out; British Gas announced extensive job
cuts

Hard Times

'That's not a button, .
it's a hard ecu'

'It's the recession—I'm
going to have to let you go'

The ERM collapsed over the summer, and John
Major suggested a 'hard ecu' in part to replace it.
Many people wondered what that was

Black Wednesday

'And now over to our economics editor'

'Wait there—we're coming up to join you'

Black Wednesday, and the pound crashes out of the ERM

Black Wednesday

'Actually, I just seek out
vulnerable currencies and
speculate against them'

'It wasn't so much the
letter as the fact that
they charged us £25 for it'

Currency speculators and the Bundesbank were
blamed for the pound's demise – though the
Bundesbank wrote to the Treasury pleading
innocence

Black Wednesday

'Sometimes I think you
don't even have an
economic strategy'

Once out of the ERM, the pound initially
plunged against foreign currencies. Could the
government come up with a new economic
policy?

Black Wednesday

'We call this the
Sterling Manoeuvre'

During the summer, there were acrobatics at the
Farnborough Air Show and on the foreign
exchanges

Still or Sparkling?

'I've got a glass of British tap water and I'm not afraid to use it'

'Goodbye cruel World'

As the French held out against a new GATT round, the quality of Britain's drinking water again came under attack

Trade Wars

'I got caught up in a fishing dispute'

In contrast to 1992, the French switched their attention from lamb to fish

Unpopular Science

'This is an ethical night-mare—I've identified the Euro-sceptic gene'

'Now you're 58 it's time to tell you the facts of life'

As the government struggled with Maastricht rebels in Parliament, scientists said that they might have identified a genetic component in homosexual behaviour. Meanwhile, a London woman of 58 said that she was pregnant as a result of fertility treatment in Italy, doctors in Britain having refused to treat her.

The Mother of All Battles

'If the American gets beaten we should get out fast'

'Room service, would you bring up two windows and an outside wall, please?'

After more border incursions by Iraq, and the discovery of a plot to assassinate George Bush, the United States lost patience and launched a cruise missile attack on Baghdad – the attack coincided with Wimbledon fortnight

The Defence Review

'Take your time, Sir Francis,
we haven't got any
ships anyway'

BOTTLE WITHOUT
A SHIP IN IT

More cuts to Britain's armed forces were
announced. The Navy took a direct hit

Trade Wars

For a time, 'British fish' was highly unpopular in France

The French government expressed reluctance to sign a new GATT round, much to the anger of the United States